FROM WHISPERS TO ECHOES: A JOURNEY THROUGH POEMS

By Lokesh Manibalan

Thirukkural (423)

"A pure heart, free from deceit, Is the foundation of all virtue."

-       **Thiruvalluvar**

Table of Contents

1) The Flower of Love…

Today, I went once again to that tree's shade,

A nameless butterfly fluttered around me.

Perhaps, drawn by the nectar

of the flower in my hand.

But today too, she did not come,

And I could not bear to let this flower wither in vain.

Nearby, an old blind woman sat in silence.

I placed the flower in her hands

And from the blossoms of her sightless eyes,

Tears of the heart began to flow.

---

2) I Died and Was Reborn…

On the stone bench

To the right of the garden,

A lone dry leaf lay still.

And beside it, I sat

And a tree stood next to me.

The three of us waited for the rain…

Between the dense, dark clouds,

A streak of lightning peeked through!

Then, from the sky - Fell the first raindrop.

It landed on a leaf of the tree beside me

And from there, splashed onto my face.

The waiting leaf drifted away.

The waiting tree was drenched.

The waiting heart within me… vanished.

In that very first drop

That the sky showered upon me,

I died, and was reborn again…

3) The Shiva Temple…

The town's Shiva temple is always bustling.

For schoolchildren, the temple tower sometimes becomes a place to leave their school bags.

On festival days, the crowd stretches in a queue far beyond the temple gates.

Sivanesan brother sets up his camphor stall, Quiet and steady, always divine.

Sakthi sister arranges her flower shop, Ties little garlands with love and care.

Vinayaka brother's ice cream cart always near— where Shivan and Shakthi meet!

and Murugan brother, with eyes full of fire, sells Tamil books—his one true desire.

Devotees step out of the temple,

banana leaves filled with holly food in their hands,

Sacred ash smeared across their foreheads.

That night, for once, mother gets a break from cooking.

As the temple prepares to close,

the crowd begins to thin.

The priest, his pockets now filled,

walks away after shutting the temple doors.

Outside, a beggar gathers the scattered water pots,

picks up the abandoned slippers,

drops them into his bag,

and finally, lying down at the temple steps,

whispers,

"Oh, my lord, Shiva!"

---

4) The Stolen sparrow

In a room overflowing with darkness,

I sat crying in silence.

Heard a soft knock echoed on the windowpane.

Hiding my tears within my eyes,

I opened the window.

Rays of light rushed in,

tearing through the darkness!

On a branch stretched near the window,

a twin-tailed sparrow swayed on its perch.

The moment it saw me,

it fluttered away.

The tears which I hid were not found,

Yet somehow,

Stolen by the sparrow.,

After that,

I never closed the window again!

---

5) She! In the early dawn

The neem blossoms softly kiss the rangoli she has drawn!

At its middle, a flower unfurls its petal-like lips!

A love-laden breeze, rising from within her to escapes to free the little ants, which are prisoned in that design!

The tender early rain drops, striving to erase the rangoli but the sun gently drank it!

On her cheeks, bright rangoli hues remain, A gentle sweat will wash them away; And for each sweat for her, This Sun awaits!

---

6) Drinking Poetry

One rainy evening,

I sat at my doorway with a tea cup in hand.

Savouring the falling rain, I sipped my tea in little mouthfuls.

When the rain paused,

A bird near me flutters, and a few raindrops brushed my face!

In that moment I realized the secrets of rain is incredible!

My neighbour's kitten drank its milk, while I enjoyed my tea;

its curious eyes seemed to ask,

"May I have some tea too?"

Yet even the cat knew his owner's permission is restricted for tea,

Meanwhile, children at play marvelled at the
rainbow blooming in the sky, and

The rainbow itself appeared to admire them!

Then one child stretched out a hand and drew
another rainbow,

A child drawn arc more precious to me than any
made by nature.

By then,

the tea in my cup was empty and

I started drinking poetry, with some raindrops!

———————————————————

7) The Real Vowels

All the moments I spent with you, now melting in my inner heat,

crumble away like droplets of tears.

You left me alone after igniting a fire in my heart.

Burning and burning,

Those moments now live only as lines on my pages!

When I feared my very life might dissolve,

I wondered! what if your memories melt away with it?

Still, I write on, laying my life upon these lines,

In the hope that someday,

you will read my very soul.

____

8) That Bygone Moment

This morning, in the shadowed courtyard,

I saw him as he was waiting for someone,

With his restrained finger,

he traced lines on the stone bench.

Nearby, the tree stirred its leaves, and

He quietly counted each falling one.

His eyes, ablaze like dancing lightning,

Wavered with unspoken memories.

The sun had already climbed to its peak,

and while watching the trembling leaves descend,

He took a towel from his shoulder

placed it upon his head

And reclined upon the bench.

At dusk, the twilight gently roused him.

I stepped near there, and he asked,

"What is the time?"

I replied, "It is now six."

Then, with a subtle, enigmatic mysterious smile,

he left that place.,

That little smile! Ah!

it was no ordinary smile to me;

In that fleeting moment,

I saw that entire bygone time reflected in his eyes!

---

9) Path Pilgrimage

Forgetting the way home, I wandered near the pond.

There I beheld the fish gliding in the water,

trees swaying in the breeze,

and waterlilies drifting along,

while the blossoms of the trees unfurled.

I watched sparrows circling above,

and water silently drank swan's thirst,

the sky itself spread over the pond,

and a frog glided gracefully by.

I even saw the sunlight drink the water,

and the water drink in the sunlight,

and countless other marvels unveiled themselves to me.

Next time, make sure that,

I must again lose the path that leads home!

10) The Painter on the Streets

In the heart of the bustling street,

an artist once painted vivid scenes-

mountains, flowers, birds,

Images that captivated the eye.

Yet, he was in no way less than the finest masters.

he painted the sky upon the ground, so that to the onlooker,

It resembled the very visage of the heavens.

Beneath that, he painted the sea,

The fish, attempting to jump from the sea to the sky,

Even every patch of the road which is appeared before,

Immersed now, lost in the boundless realms of sky and sea!

---

11) Rain

It rained again today!

As always, mother shut the doors and windows tight.

I don't know why, but this cold seems to have a strong hold on us.

The scent of rain filled the air,

My heart longed to see it. I opened the window

The damp breeze kissed my skin,

The drizzle sent shivers through me!

I unlatched the locked door,

The rain called out to me, And I went to it

Without my mother knowing!

12) A Journey Without Footsteps

I walked a silent road with no one around, tall trees stood like quiet guards.

I sat beneath one — its shade, a soft shelter.

A feather fell on me, light as a forgotten thought.

I held it, then let it go — Perhaps it was seeking the bird it once knew.

A yellow butterfly kissed a flower's lip and the flower, like a lover, held it close.

By the river, I saw colours flow —A rainbow stream painted by falling petals.

Leaves, like old stories, drifted with the current.

Then the sun rose — not just from the sky, But from the ocean of colour below.

I woke. Just a dream.

But from my 13th-floor window,

The real sun rose — Fresh from its ocean bath.

Now I step into home.

Open your doors too—Let light find its way in.

---

13) The Withered Flower

At the edge of her flowing hair,

Two hairs held a delicate flower,

Swaying in the wind, they let it fall to the ground.,

I picked it up and placed it inside a book,

Even after years,

the withered flower still longs to return to her hair.

I have come to accept that it can never happen,

But alas,

The poor withered flower does not understand...

14) A poem about the Wind

I wrote a poem,

And it drifted away in the wind.

It was about the wind, meant only for the wind,

Belonging solely to the wind.

Now,

I write again about the wind,

This time, with the window shut…

And here it is,

The poem carried by the wind,

Reaching you…

____

15) Church Feast

The church feast begins-
Sky crackers burst, lights shimmer.
Mics echo through the crowded air,

A joyous uproar, loud and bright-
Where even ears seem to shatter.

Tiny lamps encircle God, flickering soft, a glow
divine.

The feast's delight, as always, Jesus Joseph's giant
wheel -- Spinning the world topsy-turvy!

From A to Z, the festival shops Hold treasures for
every hand.

With prayers and offerings-
Debts of devotion are repaid-
As rituals unfold with grace.

Exams may loom, but children dance-
Spinning, laughing, lost in joy,

Trusting God will see them through-

"For Faith is stronger than Fear!"

Yet beyond the bells and hymns,

when the echoes fade to dust,

The lanterns dim, the laughter wanes,

And footsteps vanish in the dusk.

Wouldn't it be wonderful? if-

the glow remained,

The voices stayed,

if faith outlived the fleeting night,

like embers that never fade.

———————————————————————————

16) Just let it be.

It doesn't snow for you—

it snows for those who love the snow.

It doesn't shine for you—

it shines for those who adore the sun.

It doesn't rain for you—

it rains for those who cherish the rain.

If you love it, embrace it;

if not, then simply leave it be—

Don't blame it.

---

17) Endless Poems

I sat on the window side

For nearly two hours,

With a white sheet and

a black ink pen neatly arranged on the table.

just as they were still.,

white sheet remains blank.,

I have been reading the endless poems that

Nature keeps writing! Still!

---

18) A Cat, A Poem

The door creaked open slowly,

At First came the shadow of the cat. Soon after, that very cat, whose shadow had belonged to it, arrived.

I was seated at the far end, near the Tulsi plant on a wooden stool.

"Why has the cat come? Could it be drawn by the fragrance of the Tulsi?"

"No—it has moved toward the kitchen...

and there, alas, no milk is found!"

Then, along the very path it came, the cat departed.

Lost in thought, I wondered, "Why did it come?"

Then it hit me! Once, I had told that cat,

"I shall write a poem about you."

Yes—perhaps that is why it returned. But, oh— it left in anger!

If ever you see that cat somewhere, please say,

"Your poem and the milk are waiting!"

---

19) Little Sparrows

Not as in days gone by—

now things are different.

The fish seller next door has taken to sleeping in.
she's too late to wake up now,

In another house,

even the elderly can't seem to get up,

Aunt from opposite home clears the doorstep and
hurriedly painted a rangoli.

Meanwhile, the sparrows, who had been waiting
since dawn for their breakfast,

Fly away in disappointment –

to the next street girl's house, where maybe,

Just maybe,

Someone still remembers to feed the birds…

———————————————————————

20) City Poet

In one quiet corner of a restless metropolis-
On the 13th floor of a modest high-rise,

a poet sits by the window— writing verses of a
village

where mornings are slow, and the breeze still
knows your name.

---

21) Dreams

They ask, "What is your dream?"

But can you confine the vast ocean of dreams

onto a small piece of paper?

Can you hear the sound of a waterfall

amid the beautiful cascade of rain?

Why wouldn't you hear it! You can...

A rich man studies sitting in his apartment.

I, too, shall study—sitting on my own tent home!

Oh, my friend, Obstacles everywhere, hard work
can shatter it., Do It...

22) Unbroken

When this letter reaches you,

You may be surrounded by your son, a daughter, or even a grandchild,

Time's playful hand may have Gray your hair and wrinkles upon your face - leaving you worn by the years.

When you open this letter,

perhaps your son or daughter sits before you, quietly sipping tea;

Your grandson might call you out to play, and your granddaughter may adorn you with a garland of flowers.

When you read this letter,

The sun might be swallowed by heavy clouds,

while the scorching wind is soothed by the cool breeze of my love!

and through my writing, may the nectar of love well up in your eyes! Then, wherever I may be, I shall gather the Love!

23) The Life of Fallen Leaves

Leaves that fall from the tree

can never rejoin its branches.

The fallen leaves look longingly

at the fresh, new leaves sprouting on the tree!

---

24) A Trip Out of Town with Friends

In the heart of summer, we set out — toward a
mountain peak or the call of the sea.

Home-packed food filled our bags-- wilted idlis,
squished puris and tomato rice kissed with spice.

The road gave us flowers,

a blazing yellow sun,

a sudden rainbow, dark clouds,

and mist that clung like laughter.

Even now, those moments stay —

framed in our homes,

like soft, sunlit snapshots

that time forgot to fade.

25) The Yellow Sunshine

The sunlight entered through that window,

flowing over the ground in a scattered, almost sticky.

The aroma of the sun felt like a gentle, drowsy caress.,

That yellow light, as if painted by a master's brush, wove itself into my eyes.

No wonder, even the sun can flow like water from my eyes!

At another window's glass, the artificial hues of a fake starburst onto the ground,

while in the flowerpot by that window,

Two flowers took turns drinking the sunlight...

When the night came,

Drank the sun completely and Slept with Sweet dreams!

26) Each Memory Tells a Poem

My love, who made me a poet,

Every moment we cherished falls like verses upon
my heart.

That day, a tiny droplet of pure white, spread in the
mist of your eyes, remains, unmelted, within my
lines!

Without pause, I still see the dream we once
shared, accompanied by solitude.

When I recall those moments we walked hand in
hand,

I wonder, as if checking my fingers,

if flowers have bloomed there.

You blossom in my eyes, like pristine white blooms!

27) *You too can bring it to life!*

First, I will draw a dog.

Then, I will sketch its shadow as well.

After that, I will place it before you.

All you have to do is breathe life into it, watch as it
comes alive.,

---

28) The Saree Still Waits

Whenever I hear our song, you are the one who comes first to mind.

Though I was not born in your womb,

 I am reborn in your heart time and again.

After your marriage, you travel far, yet in spirit, you always return close.

Your marriage day,

I blossomed in your eyes; today, you bloom in mine!

After you left, even the rangoli size became small,

Your old sarees are waiting for you here,

And from your treasured ornament, a lost gem now rises—

yearning for you,

just as I do.

---

29) A Delirious/Crazy State

Outside the room where light has vanished,

The buzz of insects and a dog's battle-like bark
resound,

while sleep is lost and a thousand thoughts flood
the depths of the mind—

a moment when the very meanings of life are being
probed.

That journey toward life places fear at the forefront.

What comes next in life?

Madness overwhelms the mind completely.

Like an ceiling electric fan, forever revolving in one
spot,

life too continues its endless cycle…

In this deep search, will the true meanings of life
ever be found?

———————————————————

30) Him

Even when miles lie between us,

our souls sit side by side.

We don't need blood to feel like family—

what we share runs deeper than that.

His sister is our sister. No explanations. No
boundaries. Just truth.

Ours is a bond that refuses labels—wild, honest,
unshaken by the world.

When he is with us,

We fear nothing. His presence is power.

But when he's missed,

even the brightest sunlight

can't hide the way

our eyes tremble in his absence.

----

31) Why Did It Happen Only to Me?

A Little flower—a delicate bloom—so slowly,

Oh so slowly!

I speak of the moment it began to fall apart…

As the wind blew, and the plant danced gently.

At that moment, the fallen flower got caught
between two leaves.

In the soft breeze, as the leaves gradually parted,

the flower tumbled down to the earth!

At that very instant, the earth shook softly!

I still cannot understand why it happened only to
me?!

____

32) The Imagined Taste of the Strawberry

Back then, I had never truly tasted a strawberry

But in my imagination, I savoured it.

That imagined strawberry was something I
adored…

Yet when I tasted a real strawberry,

I found it unappealing.

Even now,

whenever I see strawberries in the anywhere,

I end up buying and tasting them,

In the shop of dreams!

---

33) Where you are now!

The pulsating heartbeat of the core.,

In endless darkness, light scatters far and wide!

And the small ball (Earth) orbiting the Red Giant (Sun)!

The tiny dot (Moon) endlessly circles— **Where you are now!**

Within this revolving world,

There are different layers like ozone—not only that,

Your layers of mind too...

amid a realm of dewy wonder and

The deep ocean's enchantment,

Lies the land that embraces it all!

____

34) A dog's cry

I have seen that dog in our street before.

Then, one day, in another street…

Another day, in yet another street…

And now, it lies before me.

Even after its guts have been torn apart,

I can still hear its cry within me!

---

35) The Life Cycle

The sky blushed red as evening fell. We were
five—friends, seekers—walking toward a mountain
peak, not knowing what we'd find.

Under a tall, aging tree, a dog lay still.

Its eyes closed forever.,

Someone had already placed wildflowers at its
feet—a farewell from a loving soul.

Above, in the branches of that same tree, a nest
held two eggs.

One was silent. The other cracked open, slow and
soft— a grey hatchling peered out; the Sky became
more reddish!

Its breath new to this world!

One feather drifted down from the nest above,
landing on the dog—Mother bird's quiet tribute to
a soul departed.

We walked on, carrying the weight of what we'd just
witnessed!

Further ahead, we saw him—

an old man, hunched and hollow-eyed, a torn bag
over one shoulder, a stick steadying his trembling
legs.

"Where are you going?" we asked.

He moved his lips, but no words came.

He looked past us, towards the direction we came from—towards the old tree…Maybe…

Maybe he has already said his goodbye!

Only his eyes spoke: tired, searching, almost finished.

Maybe he was going to meet someone.

Maybe she was waiting.

Maybe love, even in its fading breath,

May be the Final chapter.

That night, my friends slept under the stars.

But I couldn't. I lay awake,

Thinking of the old man, the cracking egg, the silent one and the feathers that wept for the dog beneath the tree.

"Yet To Birth, The Birth, The fading, The Death, —and between them all, Love remained Silent, Still, Eternal."

---

36) Shadows

They are at the age,

when wings should sprout and take flight.

But why do they stumble, like birds with clipped
feathers, forced to struggle instead of soar?

At an age when the sky should be their only limit,

Who cages them in the shadows,

hiding their light from a world that never asked?

Why are they strangers to the scent of love,

yet experts in the taste of hatred?

They are the ones meant to fight the darkness of
our broken world—

yet they live inside it, lost, unseen, unheard.

Darkness devours those whose light we ignore.

But when they rise, they will shine

like newborn stars in a clouded sky.

And as stars bloom,

so do child labourers—

one after another,

rising from the dust.

But if we let those stars

burn out,

the night will win.

If child labourers disappear—

not into silence,

but into dreams fulfilled—

then the universe, at last,

will shine brighter.

If child labourers vanish,

The universe will shine brighter.,

37) Bloomed in Darkness, Shining in Distance

After dusk falls,

Some flowers begin to bloom...

But a night, which itself a thief,

Plucks them away in secrecy.

Those stolen flowers—

They now shine as countless stars in the sky.

And in the morning,

The scent of the night still lingers

Within the flowers that remain on the plant...

____

38) Childhood Memories

We tricked our teachers, climbed the school walls,

Jumped onto the neighbour's mango tree and

tasted stolen delights.

We held swimming contests in our beloved water
tank,

And broke Olympic records in our street games.

During school lunch breaks,

we feasted on thirty different treats,

Sharing Flavors and laughter.

We placed a peacock feather inside our books,

Fed its tiny bits of paper,

And convinced ourselves it had hatched

when we opened the book the next day.

We carved our father's signature onto exam
papers,

Carefully, without leaving a trace.

We shed fake tears before the teacher's cane could
strike,

Escaping punishments with innocent faces.

In our childhood days,

We played, sang, and danced without a worry in
the world.

Those heartwarming moments, beyond words,

Let's cherish them,

And forget our sorrows...

'

____

39) Life of a stranger in distant land

With dreams in our eyes and degrees in hand,

Fate leads us far from our homeland.

Leaving behind the warmth we knew,

Into foreign winds, we bid adieu.

The breeze carries a lonely tune,

As hearts grow weary beneath the moon.

Fast-paced days and hurried meals,

Mask the longing time reveals.

Bittersweet echoes fill our days, Memories bright, yet lost in haze.

Even the pets we left behind, Wait with love, so pure, so kind.

This is the path we walk alone,

A distant land, yet never home...

____

40) The Middle-Class Family

In the first week of every month,

Father becomes an 'Arunachalam'—a man of
wealth!

Mother's bangle walks away to the pawn shop,
whispering silent sacrifices.

For us alone, schools grant an unspoken holiday,

While our home fills with endless varieties of upma.

And so, each month drags on, Like an era in
itself…

41) The Beggar

I saw him at the temple gates,

Hands outstretched, swift and keen,

Grabbing divine food before the crowd,

As if fortune had finally leaned.

Among the devotees lost in prayer,

He bowed not to the idol above,

But to the meal placed with care.

For him, hunger was the only god,

And food, the only shrine—

A beggar's prayer, not in words,

But in every morsel divine…

42) The Soul of HER

Her touch still lingers on his fingertips,

Her scent, a quiet echo within him.

Disappearance is the law of time,

Yet in his love, she is reborn—again and again.

Flowers she once adored now rest upon her grave,

A silent tribute to a love that never fades.

He lights a candle in her memory,

And as the breeze drifts by,

It gently snuffs the flame—

And in the rising smoke, she smiles…

43) Serenity

Raindrops scatter over the dancing grass,

Earth awakens with a fragrant embrace.

A butterfly rests on a blooming bud,

As tiny flowers tilt their heads in shy wonder.

Buds turn away in blushing retreat,

While raindrops glisten on leaves like scattered gems.

Sunlight kisses the waterfalls,

As peacocks, cuckoos, and parrots sing and play.

Colours bloom in the sky,

The sea gazes in awe—

Oh, what a beauty, stealing the heart away!

---

44) A Leaf and a Light

A streetlight, hidden behind the branches,

Spills its glow in quite different.

Leaves, forgetting their own colours,

turned in shades of gold and green.

Yet, many pass without a glance,

Too hurried to see this fleeting dance.

For those who pause to admire the sight,

The light and leaves steal their gaze,

Holding them captive in silent delight…

45) Pure breeze

Sweat drips as the day's toil ends, The farmer rests beneath the tree,

Welcoming the whisper of the breeze— A cool touch, a gift from nature.

Yet no machine-made wind, No artificial chill,

Can soothe him like the air, That drifts through open fields.

He is not one to summon the wind, Nor bend it to his will. He waits, patient and still,

For nature to bring its grace!

But sometimes, he has no choice

but to feel the artificial air—

like the cold breeze in the bank,

where debts wait like silent shadows.

———————————————————

46) Moments in search of flowers

A little white flower traces circles on the pond with its gravity!

Cradling the trembling morning sun within.

The Sun spills its fragrance over the water, A silent shimmer, a golden hymn...

The day and night are actually chasing the path of wandering flowers...

____

47) A Dreams, Three Birds

A tiny bird, its fragile wings tossed by the wind,

Sings a soft cry into the air.

Hearing its call, two birds awaken within my
dream— Echoing back, their voices rise,

Flew away from my open eyes.

And then,

Like whispers set free,

Two birds slip past the window's edge,

Soaring beyond my sight,

Chasing the lonely bird into the sky…

---

48) Dear Mother

To the one who shaped our lives,

Carving us from pain into something beautiful—

A living work of art!

To her, we offer our first bow of gratitude.

Looking back on every road we crossed,

In every moment we stumbled,

It was her voice that steadied us,

Her silence that sheltered us.

Love. Care. Devotion.

Different words—but they all speak one name:
Mother.

She is the flower that never fades,

Blooming endlessly

in the quiet garden of our hearts,

watering our days

with patience, strength, and grace.

49) Frying Pan Reflections

Fresh fish, bought from the market—

Cleaned, spiced, and set to fry, As oil begins to bubble, And the kitchen fills with scent.

In the corner, inside a glass bowl,

two golden fish hovers in silence.

Their scales shimmer, but their eyes are fixed—

watching, as fate crackles in a pan—

just beyond the glass.

What do they feel?

Fear?

Recognition?

Or just the silence

of those who know

but cannot swim away?

---

50) Sun's beauty

More beautiful than the rising sun in the east,

Is the glow it rise in the west— "A golden reflection", In the window of the house next door.

The sun, admiring its own beauty,

Pauses for a fleeting glance, Gazing at its mirrored self,

Before continuing its journey across the sky…

---

51) Searching

Every word I write—Carries the weight of your memory,

My pen refuses to forget you.

The flowers I once gathered from your flowing hair may have withered,

Yet in my heart, they have taken root—Growing into an unshaken tree.

Drifting through the air,

Your scent lingers somewhere—

And so, I wander, searching...

Still... still...

---

52) **Building a New Home - Memories of the Old House**

As the old house crumbles, so does the home of the termites—Collapsing into dust.

The rats and insects, who lived rent-free for years,

Now pack up and leave, their time is over.

The two proud pillars, once standing tall like Grandpa's silvered Mustache, Fall, breaking into mere rubble.

Yet, as I look at the blueprint

Of the new home—

Built with my father's blood and sweat—

A strange joy stirs within me.

This new house is grander than the one Grandpa built,

More polished, more perfect…

Yet, even here,

The scent of the old wooden beams

Climbs up my nose, and runs wild inside my mind…

---

53) Our Daughter

More beautiful than the rainbow

That graces the sky after rain,

Is the one our daughter draws—

Colouring it with tiny hands,

Filling the paper with her dreams…

---

54) Dear Father

Father flies a kite—And that kite is us!

Higher and higher we soar,

Yet if we drift astray, He pulls the string, Guiding us
back on course.

We rise into the sky,

While he stands on the ground,

Watching us with pride…

As our first and greatest admirer…

———————————————————————

55) Grandmother's Love

I once tried to take the lone coin

Hidden in Grandma's wrinkled purse,

Only to scatter its contents.

After she was gone,

That same old purse found its way to me.

Inside, there wasn't just a single coin…

But betel leaves, slaked lime,

And a faded black-and-white photo of Grandpa!

A quiet emblem of her undying love!

56) The Unread Pages

We fold the corners of unread pages,

Promising to return—

But, sometimes, we forget them.

Now and then, those pages whisper to a stray peacock feather or

a candy wrapper left between them...

Each time we flip through the book, those unread pages gaze at us, longing…

As years roll on, only dust reads their stories.

And so, with aching corners, they live and fade away…

Forever unread…

---

57) The Death

The wind brushes against him,

But he refuses to breathe it in.

Who can search for a breath?

That has vanished into the air...

The wealthy, the powerful, the rulers—

Can any of them bring it back?

No matter how great a man is,

What is lost... remains lost.

And what sin did the firewood commit?

It burns too, alongside the corpse—

Fading into nothingness...

---

58) The flower seller

With jasmine flowers left unsold,

You weave a story, just for us—

For a moment, we become Kamal and Sridevi in
your words.

A withered flower in our hands, Yet our hearts
bloom with your warmth.

For that, dear flower seller,

Our heartfelt thanks to you…

____

59) I Am a Revolutionary

In the depths of my mind, A voice speaks—

Silent yet deafening, A voiceless one…

It commands, it controls, It binds me in unseen chains.

Yet when injustice strikes, It rises—boiling, burning, breaking…

The silent screams tear through my soul,

Demanding change, demanding fire.

It pushes me, it drives me,

It whispers ceaselessly—

"Change yourself, change society,

Change the world… Be the sacrifice!"

I am not its slave; it is not my master—

It is my friend, My truest ally.

And so, it makes me write, Again and again—

"I am a revolutionary!"

---

60) The Street Cricket

While playing cricket with friends,

A plane roars in the sky— And with it, our ball soars high!

One boy runs to catch it, Eyes fixed on the sky,

But looking at the sky, he leaves that wicket.

When the rain starts pouring, our shirts and bats soak too, Yet we refuse to stop,

Rubbing spit on the wet ball,

Determined to bowl one more time.

When the ball tears apart,

One boy says, "Let's stop for today."

Another says, "We'll play again tomorrow."

But one insists,

"We can still play with the torn ball!"

---

61) The Wedding Hall and Life

At the entrance— Banana trees, mango leaf garlands,

Flower girls sprinkling rose water.

Faces beam with pride, gazing at banners of scholars Who once studied, now celebrated…

The hall gleams in golden light,

A puppet man amuses the children,

Holy smoke rises from the fire pit,

The drums echo loud.

In her eyes—tears.

On her lips—a blooming smile.

By dusk, the hall falls silent.

Scattered flowers whisper stories:

"A thousand years of harvest begin today."

———————————————

62) Deepavali

Oil baths drip down our foreheads,

While sweets tempt our hands—

But flies steal the first taste!

Smoke rises, Sparks fly,

Crackers burst into the night.

The fire on new clothes—

A mishap we rush to hide, With a hundred clever excuses!

Children keep bursting firecrackers, not knowing why—

Lighting up the crackers, which brought from

From the Narakasura fireworks store!

63) The Crow

Only the rice served for Grandpa has been
emptied.

But the potato fry I placed still remains.

I stood there, wondering why…?

"Ka… Ka…" echoed Grandma's voice!

64) Father Abroad

He left for a foreign land the moment I was born.

The first time I saw his face was in a photograph.

He kept sending money— for our education, for our home, for everything we needed!

So that poverty wouldn't touch us,

He fought against it, every single moment.

He promised to return once his work was done.

With eager eyes, we waited…

But when he came back,

He was not the face in the photograph—

Time has changed his entire looks!

____

65) Dogs

A stray dog roams freely in the streets—

a freedom a pet dog will never know.

A stray dog longs for food,

while a pet dog leaves behind leftover milk and bread.

Does the pet dog, sitting inside a car, understand the fate of a stray dog caught under its wheels?

A pet dog, circling only its home, will never know the friendships of strays.

And a stray dog, barking at midnight,

will never know the peaceful sleep of a pet dog…

————————————————————

66) Dad's old car

Father was the first to buy a car in our village—

it drew everyone's envious eyes.

Now and then, sparrows and crows would turn our
car into their restroom.

To prevent accidents, tiny god, sat inside as our
guardian.

On dust-covered windows, we traced our names,
playing with the dirt.

Without wings, it once soared through the roads,

crossing countless bumps and potholes.

Now, that very car lies abandoned in a corner,

carrying only our names,

looking at us like an orphan…

____

67) The Silent Garden of Children

As I stepped into the orphanage, it felt like walking into a withered garden.

Like once-thriving plants that had wilted, these children, meant to bloom with laughter, had forgotten how to smile...

Love is the powerful thing that has the power to make them blossom again...

In their eyes, longing whispered an unspoken pain,

searching for affection.

When we brought them food,

they smiled and said, "Thank you."

But do we need words? Isn't a smile enough?

As I stepped outside,

another child stood at the gate—

eyes filled with yearning,

lips curved into a quiet smile...

---

68) The Bicycle Tire

The bicycle tires my grandfather rode

Was our very first vehicle.

With friends, we rolled it down the street,

Our knees scraping, the tire spinning—

Racing, running, chasing one another.

When we tripped and fell, our knees bled red,

Yet we smeared mud as medicine,

Rose again, determined to outrun our friends.

The old bicycle and its tire Still remain safe to this day… But the one who rode them—

Grandfather—is no longer here.

---

69) Vegetables

After buying the vegetables

And dropping them into the bag,

A fight begins inside!

The green chili tries to stop it,

But the potato has already crushed the tomato.

Her friend, the onion, has started to weep.

A broken okra lies to one side, Exhausted...

Meanwhile, coriander and curry leaves,

Which arrived as a bonus,

Are lost in their own little love story!

70) The Farmer

The fertile fields—

All lie within your hands!

With bulls that embrace the Plow,

You till the soil, Sow the seeds,

And watch them grow! As the sky pours its rain,

A bright smile blooms on your face!

The food we eat, the life we live—

All stand as proof

Of your tireless labour!

___

71) A Daughter – A Sister

Even before my daughter was born,

I had already felt her love—through you!

Swinging high on the banyan tree,

Falling down, running to me,

Calling out "brother!" with a runny nose.

Holding my hand, Savouring a candy stick,

You walked beside me. You played mischief,

You sang like a nightingale!

Then you grew up, and distance took root.

On your wedding day,

I felt the warmth of the tears in your eyes…

And today, I feel it in mine.

---

72) The Neem Tree

It grew alongside me—The neem tree at our
doorstep!

Its blossoms adorned my mother's rangoli,

Adding beauty to her art.

Our teacher would use its twigs to punish us,

While we chewed its bitter fruit but little sweet too!

Turning the seeds into coins in our games.

Mother plucked its leaves,

Scattering them around to ward off the evil eye...

Yet, she forgot to ward off the evil eyes of the tree
itself...

Perhaps that's why, When the road was widened,

They cut it down—alive.

Even now, whenever I see a neem tree,
I remember the tangy curry which Mother made
using neem flowers , And the neem that once stood
guard-(god) over our home...

---

73) The Elevated ones

If a man, you bow in respect—

If a woman, you let her drift like a wave.

Yet, we—born of both man and woman—

Are buried without a second thought, Erased without guilt.

We have Mustaches, we have grace.

No anger, no sorrow. No hatred, only boundless love!

Yet, why do you refuse to accept us?

Do not fear!

We, too, are elevated human beings.

Show us love—

And we will give you even our very lives!

74) My Village

As we return from distant lands,

The great banyan tree welcomes us home.

The fragrance of the village lingers in the air,

The dirt roads long for our footsteps,

Dust rises in joy at our arrival.

The scent of mom's tea searches for us,

While gangs of village youths march the streets
with pride—reunite

Seeing the ties of our blood,

Our hearts drown in tears of emotion.

Floating in paradise on earth—

That is our village, our home!

———————————————————————————

75) A Little Girl's Fulfilled Wishes

She wants to swing from the sky, Dipping her feet
into the ocean's waves.

She dreams of wearing garlands Made from the
clouds that bloom above.

She wishes for dresses woven from flowers,

And a winged horse to carry her through the village.

Each day, she longs for a different star

To adorn her forehead like a sacred dot.

She yearns to swim in the moonlight,

To let her these all dreams never end.

Unfulfilled Desires: -

A kite that flies in the sky,

And the education that never gives up.,

A small clay house, Thatched with palm leaves.

Clothes without tears,

Food for three meals a day.

For dreams like these,

She prays for nights that never end...

---

76) The Ocean

From within you, the rain is born,

From within you, the sun rises!

You spit a salt, yet gift us pearls.

What are the melodies of your waves?

Your waves cool us down, you make us forget our worries.

You unite countless lovers, but who is your beloved?

For whom do you restlessly wander? Will you ever find peace?

The sun, who loves you one-sidedly, Arrives at your shores—

What do you whisper to send him away,

Leaving him to weep behind dark clouds?

Yet, you are the one—Who wipes away sun's tears too in return. You are a wonder, you are rare—

Not just the sun,

Even we fail to truly understand you!

---

77) Road Accident

"They passed away on Vaikunta Ekadashi - a
divine day; surely, they have reached heaven,"

Some murmured in the crowd.

Their bodies drifted in pools of blood,

As crows pecked at a lifeless brain.

The onlookers' stomachs churned, Yet his wife's
gut had already been wrenched by grief.

The roadside flowers, swaying in sorrow,

Whispered with the shattered heart of their innocent
child...

---

78) Unpublished poetry

Countless poems are still unpublished,

Still rolling in the dust of the earth.

Eager to rise, they are buried deep

Beneath a new writer's self-doubt.

His words wander aimlessly, confined to wrinkled pages.

They gaze back at him with longing,

Until, at last, they drown

In the depths of poet's own tears...

----

79) The Princess

"When the prince whisked me away, I woke up!

A mosquito bit my neck—was it all just a dream?"

She finishes writing,

A princess living in a small hut.

---

80) Drivers – Saviours

Even the wind rests in the hush of night, but he drifts on, eyes heavy with miles.

The road hums beneath his weary wheels, a silent witness to stories untold, to journeys that vanish with the dawn.

Tire tracks fade like fleeting echoes, yet the road remembers his touch

- a lone traveller, carving paths unseen, a shadow swallowed by distance.

The machine hums in quiet devotion, never once forsaking its keeper and

he, in turn, with hands like iron, guides it gently through the dark.

The roadside flowers bow as he passes,

petals swaying in whispered praise.

Let us, too, pause for a moment-

honouring the one who never stops,

before we, too, disappear into the road.

____

81) The Train

Before dawn and after sunrise,

The long train in its blue shirt whistles its way.

It saves the poor man's money and the rich man's time.

With its own track and its own flag, it moves alone but carries millions.

It makes forgotten hearts fly, along with window-side melodies and soaring birds.

The railway tracks, full of a million stories, Bear the scars of the train's journey.

For some, the train marks the beginning of life,

For others, it marks the end.

Despite carrying countless travellers,

The train's favourite sight remains—

A baby swinging in its mother's saree cradle…

———————————————————

82) The Search

It was around one o'clock at midnight,

At the city bus station—

Vendors were selling ginger tea, chickpea, and roasted gram,

A few food carts were still open.

Some people lay asleep on the platform, along with a few stray dogs.

While everyone was busy with their own searches,

I, too, moved forward in pursuit of mine.

The person sitting beside me in the bus

Had lost his bag. He seemed deeply troubled.

Perhaps the thief was also lost in his own search…

With a sigh, the man said,

"It feels like searching will become my whole life…"

Yes, isn't life itself just a search?!

____

83) A Final Request...

Plant small trees near my grave,

Let them grow tall and free.

As flowers, as fruits,

As leaves, as seeds,

As dust, as life—

I will rise again...

---

84) The Puzzle of the Portrait

On a white paper

I drew your eyes, Tears dripped.

I drew your lips, A Silent gave a kiss.

I sketched your brows,

My hands turned to sweat.

I traced your nose, Paper got angry.

After drawing your ears, Poems began to listen.

The strands thickened,

Completeness was achieved.

That beautiful face,

I have never seen before—

It is the lover of my thoughts!

---

85) A Paper Boat

A little fish,

leapt in joy and

wrote a poem upon the river.

From the flick of its tail,

a tiny wave was born—

but when it touched the ocean,

it became the great wave.

It swallowed the coastal city.

Streets turned into rivers.

Doors of homes—

now lifeboats of the drowning.

People clung to them,

yet not all reached the shore…

A child wept for its mother's milk.

But the mother had no food, no milk-

not even words to soothe the hunger.

And somewhere, far away,

a page from a Tamil book,

folded by tiny fingers,

once a dream of delight,

now a tattered memory,

drifted with the waves—

a paper boat…

---

86) A Cat's Gift

There, a cat…

Silent beneath the rainbow tree,

Gazing at a bird soaring aimlessly

Across the blue paper sky,

It slowly swayed its tail.

Can one fly with just a tail?

The black cat tried!

The sky stirred ever so slightly,

And the wind traced

A gentle ripple in its magical eyes.

As the colours of the rainbow

Reflected in the cat's golden eyes,

It gleamed like the heart of the sun.

From where the bird had flown,

A single feather

Drifted lazily to the ground.

Yes…

The bird had left behind

Just one feather—

A gift for the cat!

____

To You, My Dear Reader

You didn't just read the book—

You were here.

In every word,

In every silence.

Thank you for pausing with these words,

For carrying their weight,

And for walking this path,

And poem at a time.